The Science of Kindness

Contents

1 The power of kind	2
2 What is kindness?	4
3 Be kind to others	14
4 Be kind to yourself	24
5 Kindness can change the world	34
Glossary	44
Index	45
See how your actions affect others	46

Written by Laura Baker

Illustrated by Steve Evans

Collins

1 The power of kind

Think about how you feel when someone is kind to you. Do you feel good? Now think about how you feel when you are kind to someone else. Does it give you an **intense** feeling of warmth inside? That's the amazing effect of kindness!

Of course we don't help others just for our own **benefit**. But it's a pretty cool side effect!

Science has shown that being kind can:

- ✓ increase your happiness
- ✓ help you live a longer life
- ✓ improve your heart's health
- ✓ help you make friends and connections
- ✓ make others feel these effects too.

Are you ready to power up your mind?
Let's dive into the science of kindness!

2 What is kindness?

Kindness can be a kind word, a kind action or even a kind thought. It can be as small as smiling at a friend at school or as big as helping to protect the planet. Someone who is kind is generous, friendly and **considerate** to others. They are also kind to themselves!

Kind action

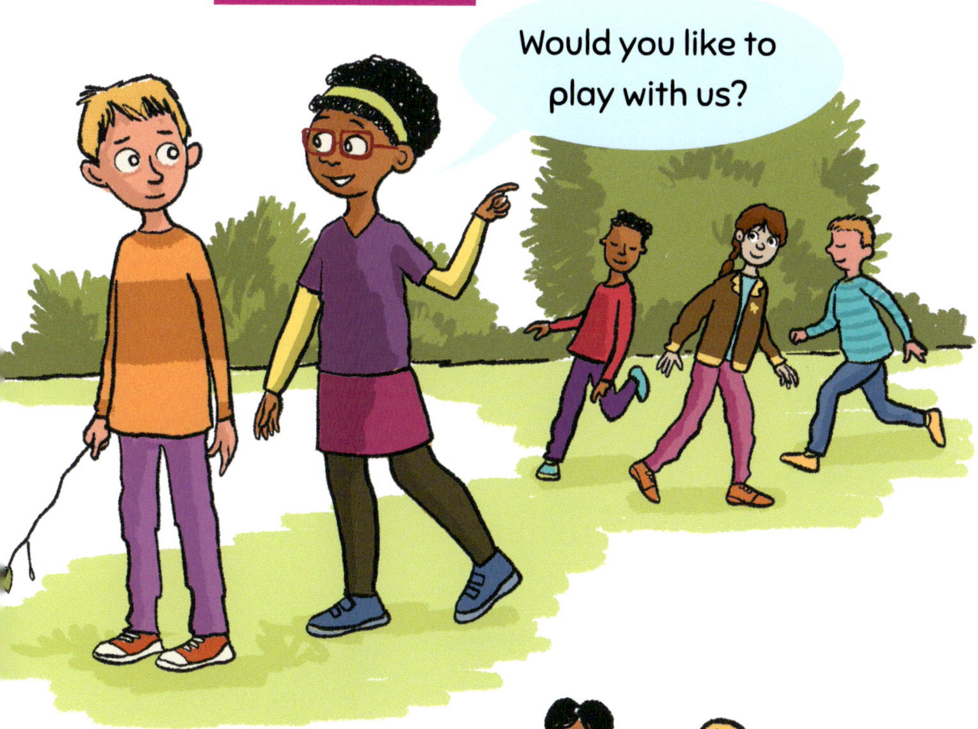

What would you do here?

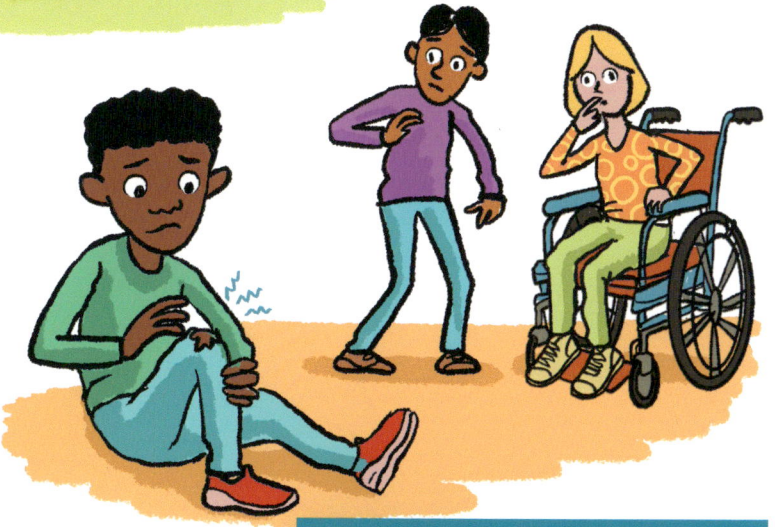

Where does kindness come from?

Throughout history, people have tried to follow the 'golden rule':

> Treat others how you hope they would treat you.

If you remember that you would like to be treated with kindness, you are more likely to treat others in this way too.

To follow the golden rule, humans need a quality known as **empathy**. Empathy is the ability to understand what someone else is feeling by imagining yourself in their situation. If you see a friend trip over at school, you can imagine how you'd feel if you tripped over too. You know you'd feel upset, so you are more likely to help your friend rather than make fun of them.

Did you know?

Variations on the golden rule have been traced as far back as Ancient Egypt. Similar ideas have been found across the world, such as in records from Ancient Greece, India, Persia and China!

Kindness and your brain

People who are kind often experience something called the 'helper's high'. This is a feeling of super-happiness; a warm glow that makes them feel buzzy and light. But why does this happen?

Scientists have discovered that when a person is kind, the brain releases **chemicals** called **hormones**. These hormones improve the person's mood, increase their confidence and even help them feel more connected to others.

A hormone called **dopamine** is responsible for the helper's high. It makes you feel good when you do something good.

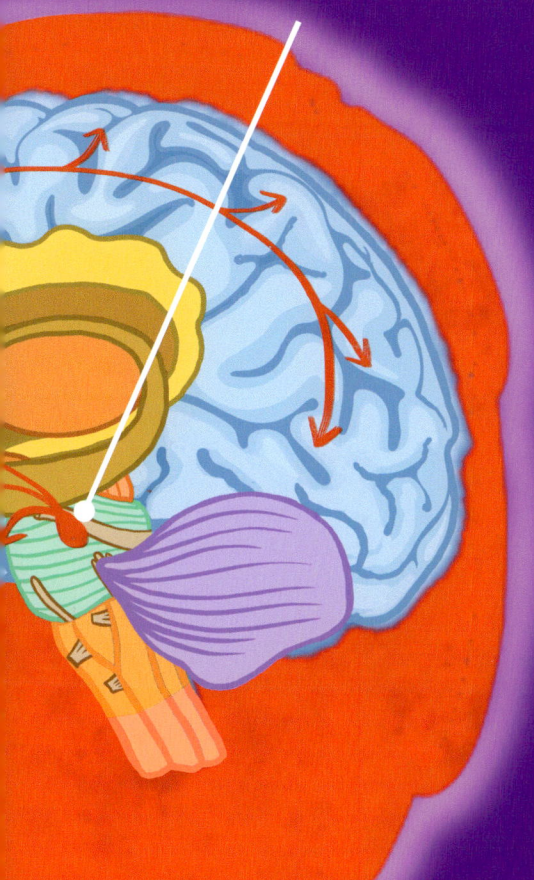

Dopamine is released in the human brain.

Did you know?

Kindness is so good for our **wellbeing** that it is used as a treatment to help people who are struggling with their **mental health**. To treat depression and **anxiety**, some therapists suggest that their patients do acts of kindness every day.

Doing these acts helps release hormones such as dopamine, which can improve the patient's mood.

Kindness and your body

When you do something kind, the hormones released help your body too.

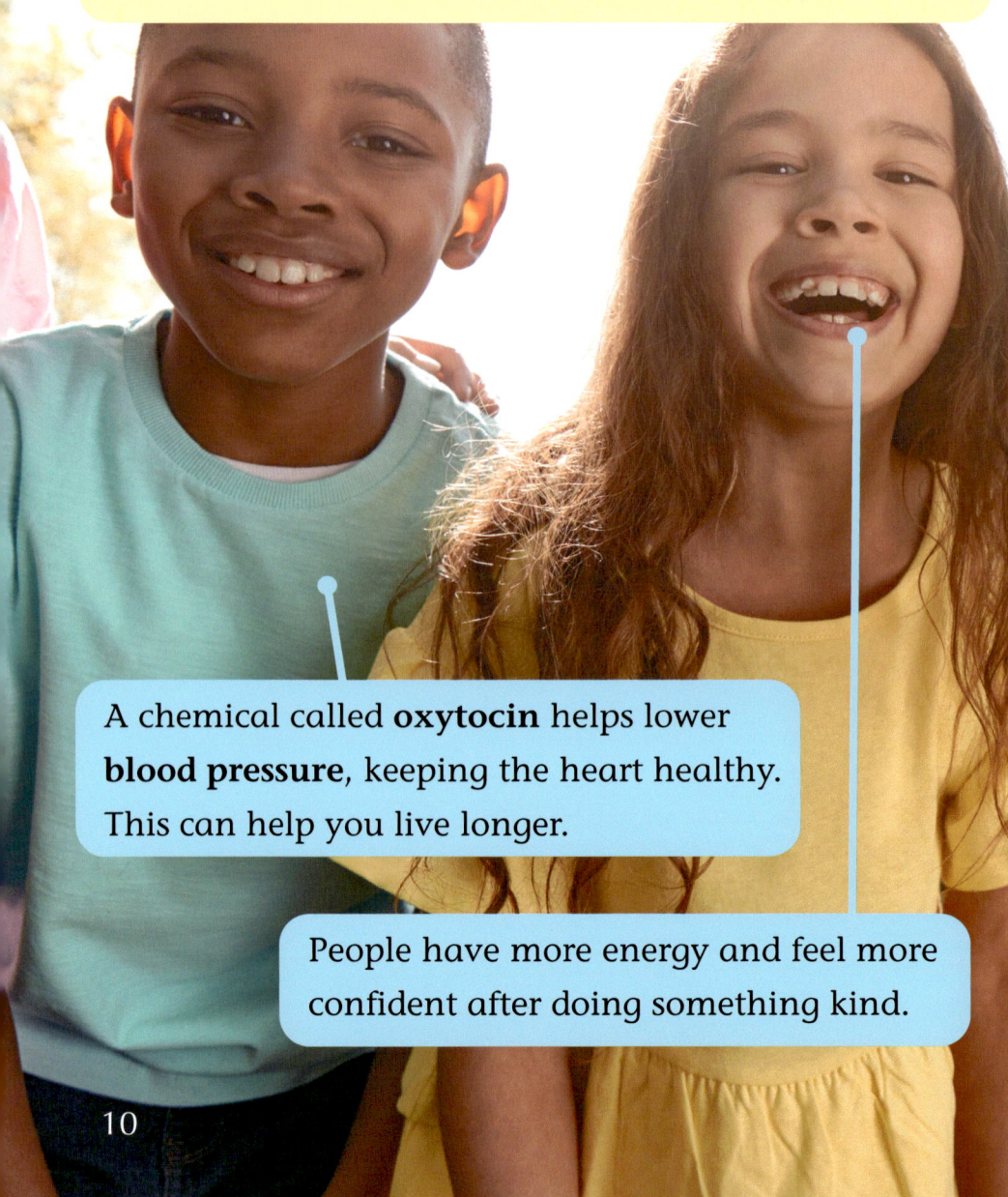

A chemical called **oxytocin** helps lower **blood pressure**, keeping the heart healthy. This can help you live longer.

People have more energy and feel more confident after doing something kind.

People who are regularly kind have less of a stress chemical than others. Stress can cause wrinkles to form more quickly, so reducing stress levels is good for the skin!

On top of that, you are passing on these benefits to someone else. If they feel your kindness, they might experience a release of the positive chemicals too and might also go on to be kind to others.

Train your brain

The chemicals released when you do something kind don't last forever. In fact, they often last for only a few minutes.

To keep the benefits going, it's important to get into a habit of kindness. The more you act in a kind way, the more natural it will become, and the more kind acts you'll do.

You can think of kindness like a muscle that needs exercise. To build up its strength, you must train regularly.

Training Routine

✅ Do one kind thing every day for a week.

✅ Turn negative thoughts into positive thoughts.

✅ If someone is unkind, respond in a kind way. This can be tough to do, so practise it as much as you can.

3 Be kind to others

Being kind to others can mean lots of different things. It's about keeping a kind **mindset** towards whoever you meet, whether you know them or not.

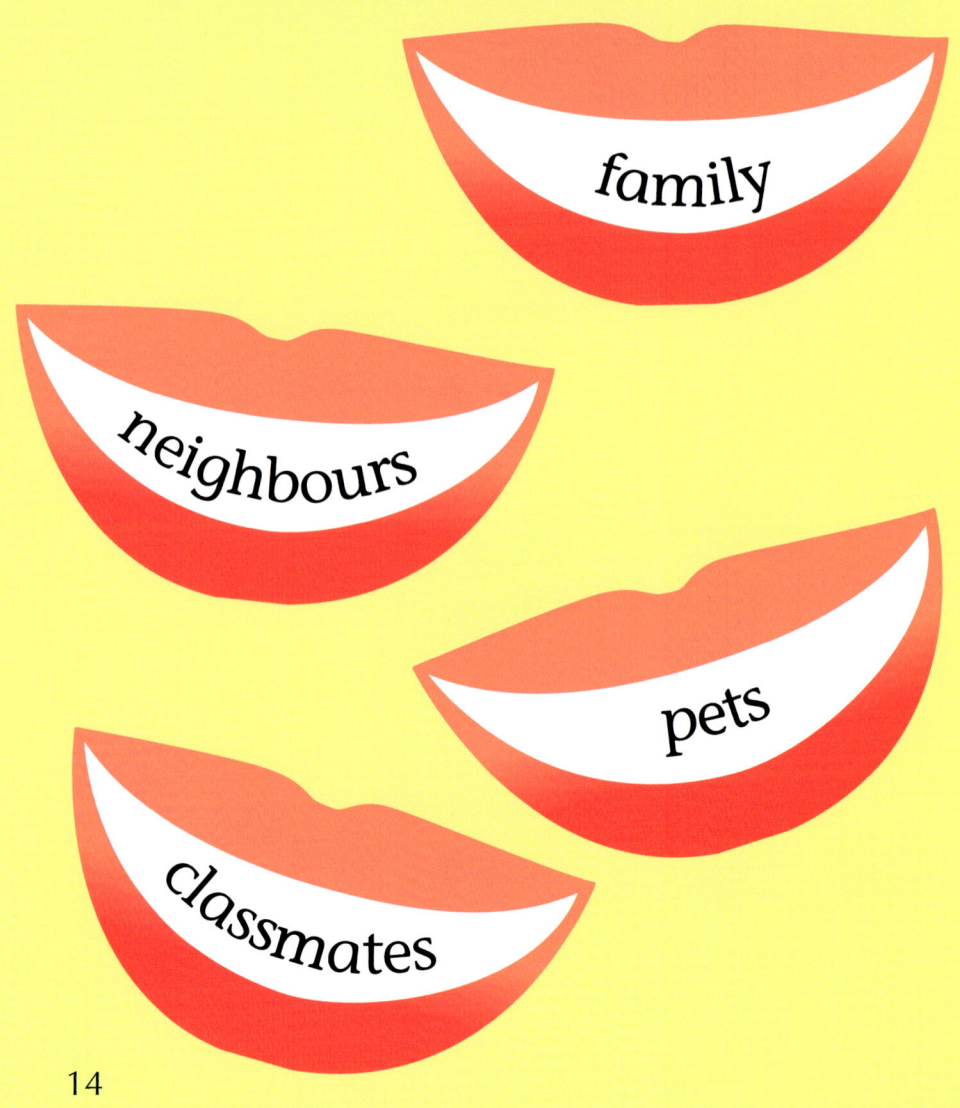

teachers

friends

tiny creatures

Chain reaction

One small act of kindness towards someone can create another … and another … and another! This is called a ripple effect or a chain reaction.

When you do something kind, the hormones released in your brain and body make you feel good.

You want to do another kind thing to feel good again!

And the chain goes on and on!

The person you are kind to has a release of these hormones too.

They want to perform an act of kindness as well.

Teach to learn

You can show kindness by helping someone else to learn. This could be by showing them how to climb a tree, encouraging them to ride a bike or helping them with work in class.

When you teach someone a skill it helps you learn that skill more deeply too. As you explain an idea, such as a maths concept, the idea becomes clearer in your own mind and reinforces your learning.

Working together and sharing ideas can also help you find even better solutions than you might come up with on your own. Teamwork makes the dream work!

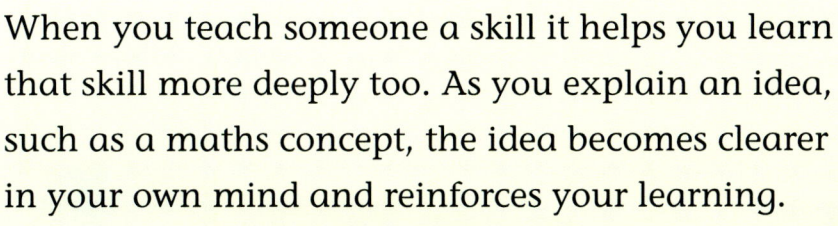

Connect with kindness

Remember the chemical oxytocin that is released when you do something kind? As well as helping your heart and body, this clever chemical also helps with social bonds: connections with other people.

When oxytocin is released, you feel more trusting of others, more generous and even friendlier than before. This means that when you are kind to someone else, you connect with them and might even make a new friend!

As kindness spreads, the world becomes more connected.

Random acts

An important part of kindness is that you do it **selflessly** without expecting anything in return.

Random acts of kindness are small gestures that people don't expect. They can make people feel good, happy and loved. Here are some random acts that you can try:

holding a door for someone

really listening to a friend, without interrupting

putting out food for birds

playing with a pet

sending a
handwritten note

tidying a shared
room in your house

making a cold drink for
someone on a hot day

asking someone if
they would like a hug

making someone laugh

telling someone what
you like about them

baking someone
a cake

Can you think
of others?

4 Be kind to yourself

Never forget one important person who deserves kindness: you!

Sometimes we can be so busy that we forget to be kind to ourselves. Try treating yourself like you would treat your best friend: with kindness and respect.

If you are kind to yourself, you will be happier, more confident and in a better mindset to help others. It all connects!

Choose happy!

Why should I be kind to myself?

It is very important to take care of your own wellbeing. Wellbeing is the feeling of being happy, comfortable and healthy. If you are in a good state of mind, you will be more able to deal with anything that comes your way.

When you are kind to yourself, you improve your wellbeing. For example, if you always tell yourself that you can't do something, you might begin to believe it. But if you give yourself a chance and tell yourself you CAN, you might believe that instead!

Be kind to your mind

When you practise self-kindness, you are being kind to your mind.

Being kind to yourself can improve your **self-esteem** – the confidence that you have in yourself and your abilities. It can make you less likely to criticise yourself and more likely to be gentle with yourself.

This self-kindness can help you deal with times when you feel stressed or anxious. It all comes back to the extraordinary power of being kind!

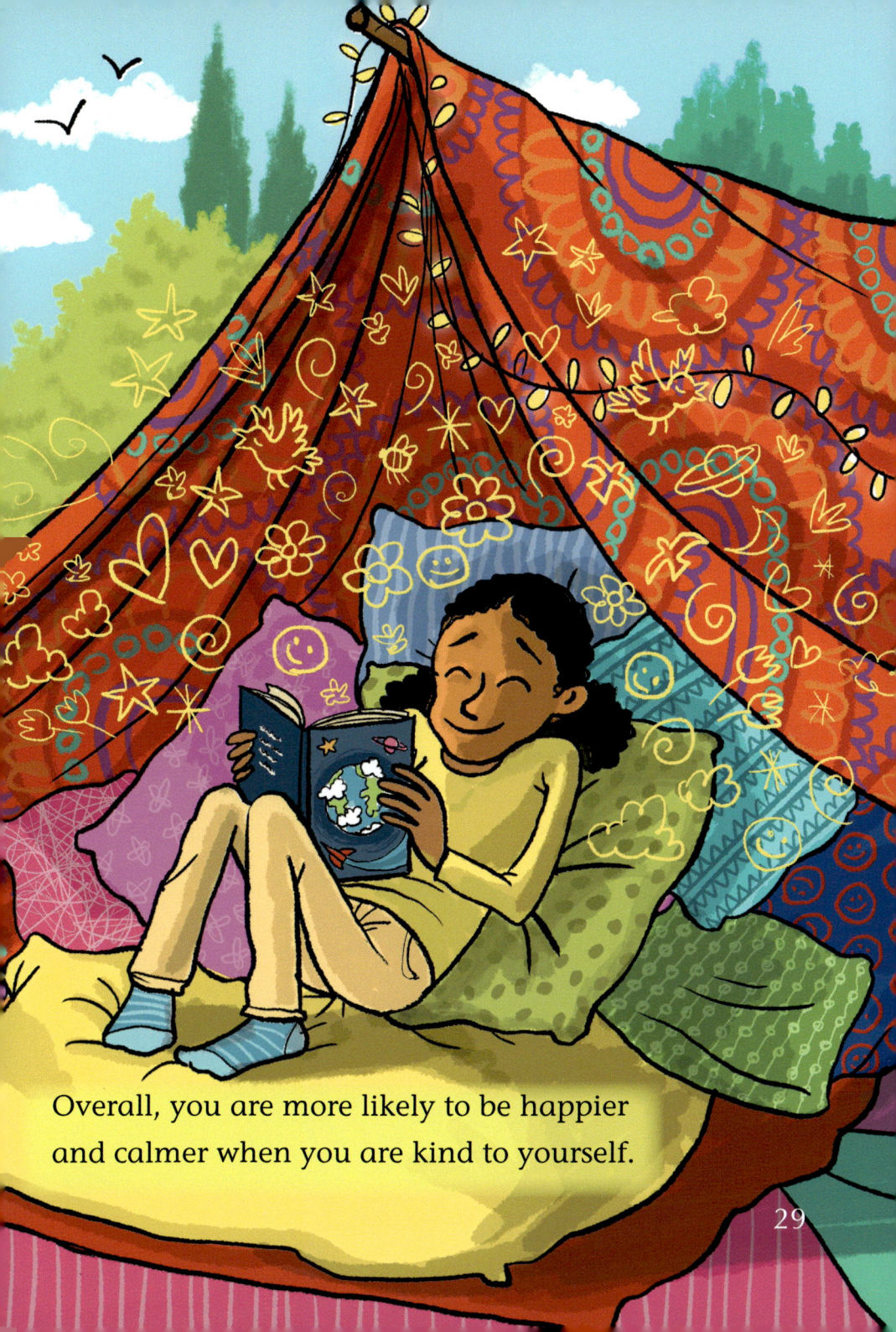

Overall, you are more likely to be happier and calmer when you are kind to yourself.

Practise self-care

Being kind to yourself is just like being kind to others: it can include a kind thought, a kind word or a kind action.

Here are some ways that you can be kind to yourself. Can you think of others? Reflect on what makes you feel happy and calm.

Say three nice things to your reflection in a mirror.

Tell yourself it's alright if something doesn't go to plan.

Stop and listen to your feelings.

Ask for help.

Take time out to chill.

When someone is unkind

You can't control whether other people are kind. What you can control is how you react to unkindness.

Imagine a friend is shouting at you because they want the same ball that you want when you're playing. Do you shout back? That would be meeting unkindness with unkindness.

Try these techniques when someone is unkind to you.

- ✅ Stay calm. Take a deep breath.

- ✅ Walk away if you can.

- ✅ If you need to respond, do it calmly. Don't raise your voice.

- ✅ Take time to think. Remember to react with empathy: Why might this person be acting in this way? How can you help them or react in a positive way?

It can be very difficult to keep calm in the face of unkindness, but practise keeping your cool and it will become easier.

5 Kindness can change the world

It is easy to think that one person can't make a difference on their own, but there are many examples of people who have changed the world with acts of kindness.

Orion Jean founded 'Race to Kindness' when he was just 9 years old, collecting and donating books, meals and toys for his **community** and beyond. Schoolgirl Greta Thunberg stood up for climate change and inspired a whole movement of people to fight for the planet.

From recycling rubbish at home to cleaning up a town park to raising awareness to bring education to all, one small act can make a big difference.

Orion Jean

Greta Thunberg

Start small

The most important thing you can do is start somewhere. Think of the ripple effect. If you are kind to three people, those three people are likely to be kind to three people themselves. Then those people will pass on the kindness too, and soon your one small act might have spread to dozens of people making a positive change!

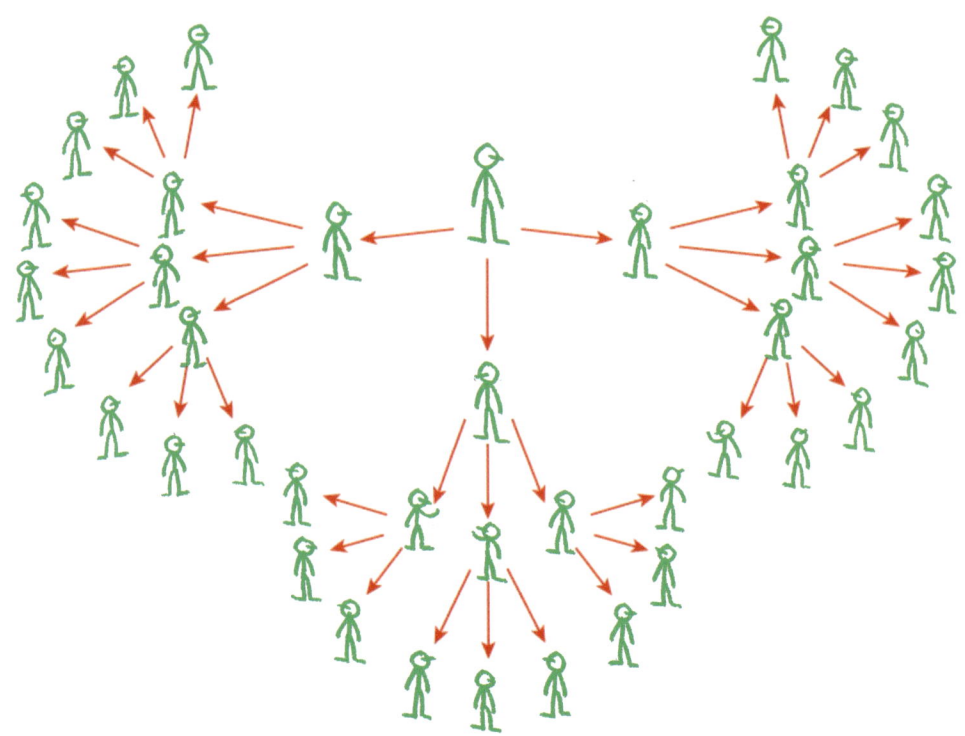

And the chain goes on!

You might also find that when you start taking action, other people will join in and follow your lead.
By focusing on what you can do, you can make your own change in the world.

Did you know?

Some scientists believe that kindness has helped the human species survive. By working together, we have built a **society** that has overcome many obstacles and stands strong today. It is when people are unkind and do not have empathy that conflicts break out.

What can I do?

Think about what matters to you. When you help a cause you care about, you not only benefit that cause but also your own wellbeing.

There are many ways to get involved. For example:

- Make a poster to raise awareness of your cause.

- Plan a fundraising event for the cause, such as a bake sale. You could also join a local community event if there's one nearby.

- Do as you say! For example, if you're fighting for the planet, cut down on your own rubbish, turn off the lights when you're not using them and use reusable water bottles and bags.

Case study

When artist Michael Landy was travelling on the London Underground, he spotted two strangers helping each other. He began to wonder why people might choose to be kind instead of keeping to themselves.

This moment inspired him to create an art project called *Acts of Kindness*. His art showed the connection of one person to others. It also shared short stories of kindness. Michael wanted people who saw the pieces to think of their own connections and shared experiences.

His work was displayed in many of the Central Line underground stations and trains in London from 2011 to 2012.

What do you think?

What do you think the art means? Could people passing by it be inspired to be kind too?

Acts of Kindness by Michael Landy

Stay kind

When the world seems too much, or life feels tricky, don't give in to fear. Instead, choose kindness. By living each day with kindness in mind, you can spread kindness at home, at school and in your community too. You might even change the world!

And as you make a change to the world outside, you'll feel the biggest change inside. Your happiness will swell, your confidence will grow and your energy will soar. Your body and mind will thank you!

Glossary

anxiety — a feeling of worry or nervousness about something

benefit — gaining something positive from something

blood pressure — the pressure of blood in the body, used to measure the heart's health

chemicals — substances that are always made up in the same way, in nature and by humans

community — a group of people who live in the same place or who have something in common

considerate — being careful not to harm or bother others

dopamine — a hormone released in the brain, responsible for the 'helper's high'

empathy — the ability to understand and share the feelings of others

hormones — chemicals that take messages from one part of the body to another

intense — strong, when talking about emotions and feelings

mental health   a person's emotional health

mindset   a person's set of beliefs about themselves and the world around them

oxytocin   a chemical released by the body

self-esteem   a person's confidence in themselves

selflessly   acting in a way that thinks about others and not yourself

society   people who share a community

wellbeing   being comfortable, happy or healthy

Index

Acts of Kindness (art) 40–41
Ancient Egypt 7
chain reaction 16–17
empathy 6, 33, 37
golden rule 6–7
helper's high 8
Jean, Orion 34–35
Landy, Michael 40–41
London Underground 40–41

oxytocin 10, 20–21
random acts of kindness 22–23
ripple effect 16, 36
self-care 30–31
stress 11, 28
Thunberg, Greta 34–35
unkindness 13, 32–33, 37
wellbeing 9, 26, 38

See how your actions affect others

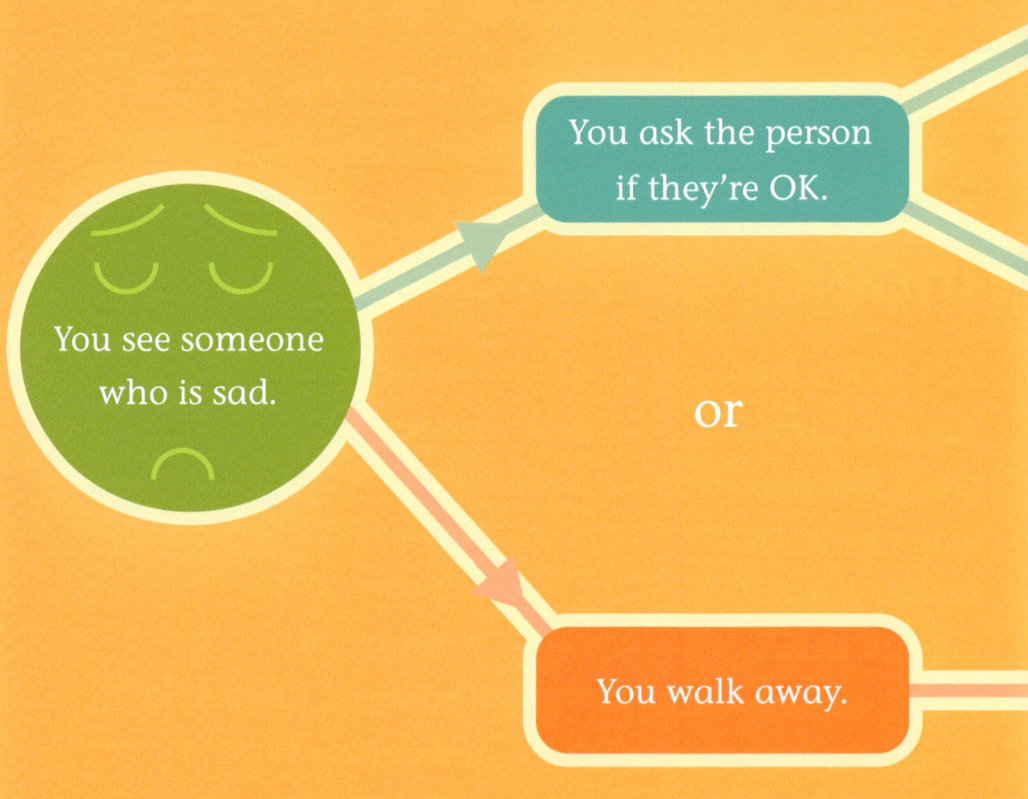

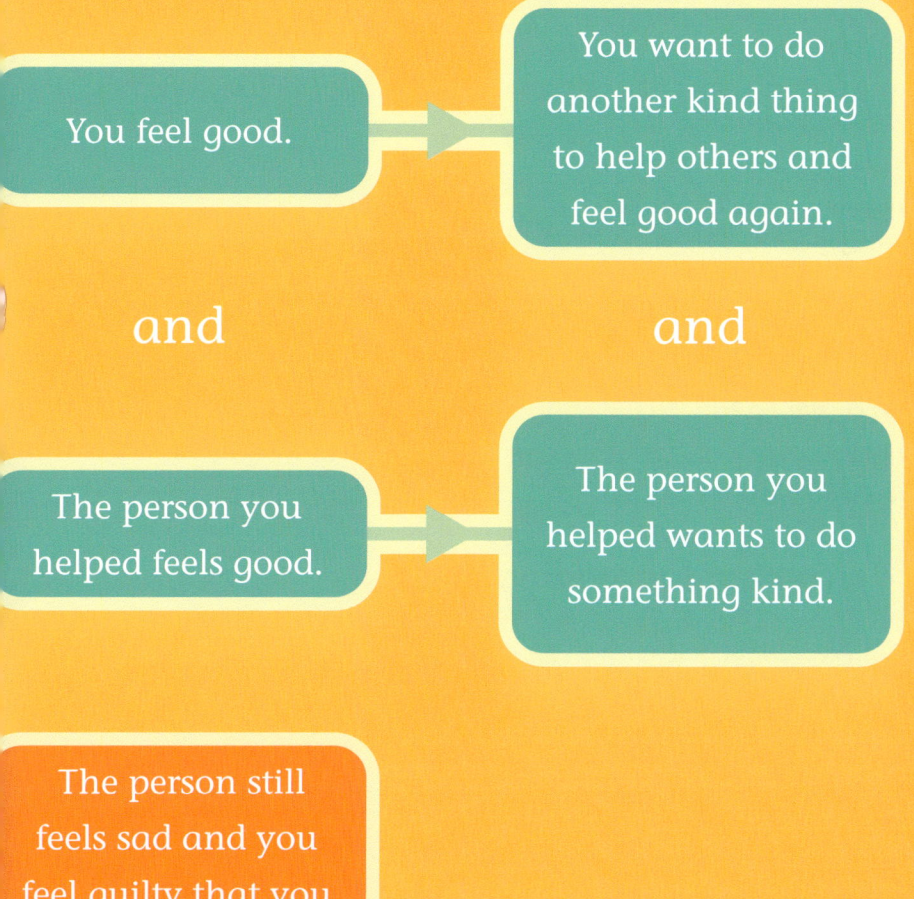

Ideas for reading

Written by Gill Matthews
Primary Literacy Consultant

Reading objectives:
- be introduced to non-fiction books that are structured in different ways
- discuss and clarify the meanings of words, linking new meanings to known vocabulary
- answer and ask questions

Spoken language objectives:
- participate in discussion
- speculate, hypothesise, imagine and explore ideas through talk
- ask relevant questions

Curriculum links: Relationships education: Caring friendships

Word count: 2526

Interest words: kind, generous, confident, trusting

Resources: paper and pens

Build a context for reading

- Ask children to look at the front cover and to read the title. Discuss kindness, exploring what the children think it is and how they think it is shown.
- Read the back cover blurb. Ask how this has helped them to understand more about the topic of the book.
- Point out that this is an information book. Ask children what features they expect to find in the book.
- Give them a few minutes to skim through the book to find some of these features.
- Ask children to find the contents page. Discuss the purpose and organisation of a contents.